A Note From Rick Renner

I am on a personal quest to see a "revival of the Bible" so people can establish their lives on a firm foundation that will stand strong and endure the test when the end-time storm winds begin to intensify.

In order to experience a revival of the Bible in your personal life, it is important to take time each day to read, receive, and apply its truths to your life. James tells us that if we will continue in the perfect law of liberty — refusing to be forgetful hearers but determined to be doers — we will be blessed in our ways. As you watch or listen to the programs in this series and work through this corresponding study guide, I trust that you will search the Scriptures and allow the Holy Spirit to help you hear something new from God's Word that applies specifically to your life. I encourage you to be a doer of the Word that He reveals to you. Whatever the cost, I assure you — it will be worth it.

> Thy words were found, and I did eat them;
> and thy word was unto me the joy and rejoicing of mine heart:
> for I am called by thy name, O Lord God of hosts.
> — Jeremiah 15:16

Your brother and friend in Jesus Christ,

Rick Renner

Questions and Answers With Rick Renner

Copyright © 2020 by Rick Renner
8316 E. 73rd St.
Tulsa, Oklahoma 74133

Published by Rick Renner Ministries
www.renner.org

ISBN 13: 978-1-68031-806-7

eBook ISBN 13: 978-1-68031-807-4

How To Use This Study Guide

This five-lesson study guide corresponds to *"Questions and Answers With Rick Renner"* (Renner TV). Each lesson in this study guide covers a topic that is addressed during the program series, with questions and references supplied to draw you deeper into your own private study of the Scriptures on this subject.

To derive the most benefit from this study guide, consider the following:

First, watch or listen to the program prior to working through the corresponding lesson in this guide. (Programs can also be viewed at **renner.org** by clicking on the Media/Archives links.)

Second, take the time to look up the scriptures included in each lesson. Prayerfully consider their application to your own life.

Third, use a journal or notebook to make note of your answers to each lesson's Study Questions and Practical Application challenges.

Fourth, invest specific time in prayer and in the Word of God to consult with the Holy Spirit. Write down the scriptures or insights He reveals to you.

Finally, take action! Whatever the Lord tells you to do according to His Word, do it.

A few of the resources Rick used to answer questions in the series are: *No Room for Compromise, Christmas: The Rest of the Story* study guide, and *The Coming of the Antichrist* study guide. Please visit our website to view and select from Rick's other available resources as well. You can place your order at **renner.org** or by calling 1-800-742-5593.

TOPIC
Mythology and Giants

SYNOPSIS
The five lessons in this study on *Questions and Answers With Rick Renner* will focus on the following topics:

- Mythology and Giants
- People of the Old Testament
- Answers From the Old Testament
- Angels and Monsters
- Answers From the New Testament

The emphasis of this lesson:

Just who were the "sons of God"? Were they angels, or the descendants of Seth as some have suggested? In this lesson, Rick answers these questions and shares what the Early Church leaders believed and taught on this issue and how mythology is rooted in the events of Genesis chapter 6.

There are many unique treasures and artifacts that adorn the Renner TV studio in Moscow, and one of those items is the leg bone of a woolly mammoth. During prehistoric times, the area of northern Siberia was covered with herds of woolly mammoths, and today their remains are buried in the permafrost. When the weather changes and the permafrost begins to melt, the bones and the tusks of these enormous creatures begin to burst out of the ground. People walking through the area can easily pick them up, which is exactly how the mammoth leg bone found its way into the Renner TV studio.

The mammoth remains from this creature are a powerful reminder that there are many unanswered questions about such things as prehistoric times and how dinosaurs fit into the Bible. Some things have just not been revealed to us — and that's okay. The Bible says, "The secret things belong unto the Lord our God: but those things which are revealed belong to us and to our children for ever..." (Deuteronomy 29:29).

It's true that we don't have all the answers, but we don't have to know everything to trust God and His Word. We just have to know and believe what He has revealed and build our lives on these truths. He is a Great God, worthy of our trust and our praise!

Have You Ever Wondered Who the 'Sons of God' Were?

One of the questions that many people ask is who are the "sons of God" in Genesis 6? Are they the descendants of Seth, the son of Adam? Or are they angels as some people have suggested? Although some may dismiss this question as trivial or foolish, it is actually an important question that is worth answering.

The Bible says, "And it came to pass, when men began to multiply on the face of the earth, and daughters were born unto them, that the sons of God saw the daughters of men that they were fair; and they took them wives of all which they chose" (Genesis 6:1,2). What was the result of the "sons of God" taking the daughters of men and making them their wives? We find the answer in Genesis 6:4: "There were giants in the earth in those days; and also after that, when the sons of God came in unto the daughters of men, and they bare children to them, the same became mighty men which were of old, men of renown."

This account in the first few verses of Genesis 6 is from where mythology was birthed. Rick Renner discusses this subject from his unpublished research entitled, *A Possible Historical Source for Mythology*. He shares how a large number of scholars agree that the phrase "sons of God" in Genesis 6 refers to *fallen angels*. These fallen angels literally entered the earth's atmosphere with a lustful desire to have sexual relations with women. This is precisely what was written and understood by numerous Early Church fathers and never questioned all the way into the Fifth Century.

It was during the Fifth Century AD that there was an increasing uncomfortableness about the "fallen angel" understanding of Genesis 6. It appears that the worship of angels had begun within the Church during that time, causing a number of leaders to withdraw from this long-held interpretation. In its place, some church leaders began to assert the "line of

Seth" interpretation, claiming that the phrase "sons of God" referred to the "righteous descendants of Seth"— the son born to Adam and Eve after Abel was murdered by Cain and Cain was banished to wander the earth. This "Sethite" view, which is not founded in Scripture, gained traction and prevailed into the Middle Ages. Even today, it is still taught and widely accepted in many churches.

What Did the Early Church Fathers Have To Say About the 'Sons of God'?

As we noted, Early Church fathers — and writers — believed that the phrase "sons of God" in Genesis 6 referred to *fallen angels* who came to earth and took on the form of men and then had sexual relations with human women. The offspring, or children, produced by their ungodly union were the giants. Here are some direct quotes from these leaders that confirm this fact:

St. Clement [circa 35-99 AD]

"The angels, fallen angels, changed themselves into the nature of men…yet having become in all respects men, they also partook of human lust, and being brought under its subjection they fell into cohabitation with women…. But from their unhallowed intercourse spurious men sprang forth, much greater in stature than ordinary men, whom they afterward called giants."

St. Irenaeus [circa 130-202 AD]

"For unlawful unions came about on earth, as angels linked themselves with offspring of the daughters of men, who bore to them sons, who on account of their exceeding great [size] were called giants."

Josephus [circa 37-100 AD]

"…For many angels of God accompanied with women, and begat sons that proved unjust, and despisers of all that was good, on account of the confidence they had in their own strength; for the tradition is, that these men did what resembled the acts of those whom the Grecians called giants."

Tatian [circa 110-180 AD]

"These fallen angels were captivated by the love of women and begat children who are those who are called demons."

What's interesting about Tatian is that when you read everything he wrote, you understand that this earthly invasion by fallen angels and their union with women is where all paganism began. The common theme of all ancient pagan religions is the idea that gods came to earth. The reason all these religions seem to have the same jargon is because there really was an invasion by celestial beings, and it is documented in Genesis 6.

These are the words voiced by four notable Early Church leaders. All of them believed and taught that the "sons of God" in Genesis 6 were fallen angels that had sexual relations with earthly women and produced giants. But these are not the only notable Church leaders who maintained this view. Similar statements and teachings can be found by Justin Martyr, Clement of Alexandria, Tertullian, Ambrose, Jerome, Eusebius, Augustine, and many others.

To be clear: the phrase "sons of God" in Hebrew is *B'nai HaElohim*, which would literally be translated *"Sons of Elohim."* This is the term used several times in the Old Testament for *angels*, including three times in Genesis 6 as well as in Job 1:6; 2:1; and 38:7. If the "sons of God" were actually the "sons of Seth," as some have alleged, that is the way God would have written it in Scripture — but He didn't.

Where Did Mythology Come From?

Now, when you study Greek mythology, you will find the story of Zeus and many other heavenly beings that came to earth. What's interesting is that if you trace back all of the early religions in the world, you will find that they involve the worship of these beings.

The fact is, there are massive pagan temples — or the remains of temples — all across the ancient Greek, Roman, and Egyptian worlds. If you travel to Greece, Rome, or Turkey, you will see these enormous temples that were built for the gods the people worshiped. Likewise, if you sailed up and down the Nile River, you'd see the many pyramid-shaped shrines that still dot the landscape. Knowing that the people of these civilizations were well-educated and sophisticated, it is just not reasonable that they based their religious beliefs on their overactive imaginations. There had to be a measure of validity to their stories.

It is true that we call their legends *myth*ology, but the ancient pagans didn't believe their stories were made of myths. They believed they were based in fact — that there actually were heavenly beings that got involved with women on the earth. And when these heavenly creatures "came in unto the daughters of men" (Genesis 6:4), the women gave birth to giants and demigods.

Keep in mind a very important fact: It was the Greeks that gave us things like mathematics, logic, art, architecture, and poetry. These were brilliant people and they would not have based their beliefs just on an overactive imagination. Their beliefs were rooted in the events of Genesis 6.

Just imagine if you had lived thousands of years ago and were an eye-witness to the fallen angels actually entering the earth's atmosphere. The sight of such supernatural activity would be quite impressive — even if the beings were corrupt. The point is, the people who witnessed these dazzling creatures come into the world never forgot what they saw. The experience was so branded in their memories that they retold the stories to their children and their children's children. Thus, Greek mythology finds its roots in the biblical narrative of Genesis 6.

Make no mistake: the event described in Genesis 6 is real and it actually took place. But the beings that came to earth and had relations with human women were not Zeus, Kronos, Jupiter, or any other mythological being. The creatures who came were fallen angels ("sons of God") just as Genesis 6 states, and from their union with earthly women, they gave birth to giants. It is from this biblically documented event that many legends came forth, which today we call mythology.

'Giants' Are a Big Deal in the Bible

Giants are actually mentioned in numerous places throughout the Old Testament, including the books of Genesis, Numbers, Deuteronomy, Joshua, Second Samuel, First Chronicles, and Job. In Genesis 6, the word "giants" is a translation of the Hebrew word *nephiyl*, which is from where we get the word *Nephilim* — one of the most commonly used names for "giants" in the Old Testament. It describes *a bully or tyrant; one that was physically enormous in size*, or *monstrous in stature*. These hybrid beings possessed incredible strength, which enabled them to become legendary in the earth.

The Bible is very clear that once the "giants" — *Nephilim* — were on the earth, the condition of mankind and the world was dreadful. The earth's population became so influenced by these appalling creatures, the Bible says, "And God saw that the wickedness of man was great in the earth, and that every imagination of the thoughts of his heart was only evil continually" (Genesis 6:5). Scripture goes on to say, "The earth also was corrupt before God, and the earth was filled with violence. And God looked upon the earth, and, behold, it was corrupt; for all flesh had corrupted his way upon the earth" (Genesis 6:11,12).

It is interesting to note that nowhere in the Bible does it ever say anything positive about a giant. In every passage where they are mentioned, something bad is happening. That is what we see here in Genesis 6. The giants were evil, and they had filled the earth with violence. In fact, things were so horrifying God decided to totally destroy the earth by a flood. Friend, these were the days of Noah, and God used the Great Deluge to wipe out the hybrid race of giants that were on the earth.

Now, we know from Genesis 6:4 that there were also giants on the earth *after* the flood. How they made a comeback, the Bible doesn't say. Nevertheless, a careful study of Scripture reveals that there were several tribes of giants populating the earth, including the Rephaim, Anakim (sons of Anak), Rephidim, Zuzims, and of course the Nephilim. These towering tyrants were thriving in many regions — including the Promise Land that God had given to the nation of Israel. God told Israel to eradicate the giants from the earth, and while they did wipe out many — including King Og of Bashan — some remained in the land. Goliath from Gath, whom David later defeated, is an example.

The New Testament Confirms
The Fallen Angel Account in Genesis 6

In the Writings of Peter

What is quite interesting is that both Peter and Jude refer to the event described in Genesis 6 in their New Testament writings. For example, in Second Peter 2:4, Peter wrote, "…God spared not the angels that sinned, but cast them down to hell, and delivered them into chains of darkness, to be reserved unto judgment." In this verse, the apostle Peter does not mince words. He tells us clearly that God placed the sinning angels into "chains of darkness."

The word "chains" in this verse is the Greek word *seira*, which does not refer to a physical chain. It actually depicts *an underground pit or cavern that was used to contain vicious animals* like wolves. It is the very word that was used to describe *an underground place of retention or containment*, or *a prison*.

Peter said this underground cavern or prison was filled with "darkness," which in Greek is the word *zophos*, and it describes *absolute pitch darkness that is totally void of light*. This is the type of darkness that can be felt, and it is suffocating. To be placed in a prison of suffocating darkness would be the ultimate punishment for an angel that was originally created to live in the light of the glorious presence of God.

Finally, Peter tells us that God put these rebellious angels in "hell." The word for "hell" here is the Greek word *Tartarus*, and if you know about Greek mythology, you know that *Tartarus* is the name given to describe the underworld. Specifically, it is the section of the underworld set aside for the wicked. When you hear about *Tartarus*, it is synonymous with an underground cavern, pit, or dungeon, or a subterranean chamber where rebellious gods were imprisoned. By using this word in this passage, Peter makes a connection between mythology and what occurred in Genesis 6.

In the Writings of Jude

Jude, the brother of Jesus, also commented on the events in Genesis 6 in his book. Initially, he intended to write about the wonderful salvation that we have through Christ, but with all that was going on at that time, he felt prompted by the Holy Spirit to write on more pressing matters, which included the fate of the fallen angels.

In Jude 1:6, he said, "And the angels which kept not their first estate, but left their own habitation, he hath reserved in everlasting chains under darkness unto the judgment of the great day." The word "everlasting" in Greek depicts God's *irrevocable decision* and *determination* that these rebellious angels would never escape His judgment. And to ensure that they would never escape the underground place of containment, God placed these angels in "chains." In this verse, the word "chains" describes *the chains or bonds that were reserved for the most dangerous criminals.*

In God's mind, these were criminal angels. By using this sequence of words, Jude depicts a moment in past history when God Himself reached down and seized an offending company of criminal angels and personally bound them in chains. In God's eyes their actions were so outrageous and appalling, He declared a sentence so final that there would never be negotiation for their release.

In the mouths of these two New Testament witnesses — Peter and Jude — the truth of the supernatural events of Genesis 6 were confirmed. Regardless of how exaggerated the fables of mythology have become over thousands of years, it seems unlikely that intelligent Greeks, Romans, and Egyptians would have founded their entire religious beliefs on mere fantasies. Even the Early Church fathers couldn't buy that. On the contrary, they agreed that mythology had its roots in the real-life event which is recorded in Genesis 6.

STUDY QUESTIONS

Study to shew thyself approved unto God, a workman that needeth not to be ashamed, rightly dividing the word of truth.
— 2 Timothy 2:15

1. Prior to this lesson, had you ever heard of the "sons of God" talked about in Genesis 6? What about the "giants"? If so, what did you know about them?

2. One of the renowned giants in the Old Testament is King Og of Bashan (the area just east of the Sea of Galilee and south of Damascus). Og is actually talked about in six different books of the Bible, including Deuteronomy 3:1-11. Carefully read this passage and identify:

    • Who was Og and his people fighting?

    • What was the outcome of the battle?

    • What does verse 11 say about Og?

    • If a cubit is 18 to 21 inches, how big was Og's bed?

3. Og was not the only notorious giant in Scripture. There was also Goliath from Gath whom David slew with a slingshot and a stone. What interesting fact about Goliath is mentioned in First Chronicles 20:4-8? And what physical characteristics about giants are documented?

PRACTICAL APPLICATION

**But be ye doers of the word, and not hearers only,
deceiving your own selves.
—James 1:22**

1. What new insights have you learned in this teaching regarding *giants*, *fallen angels*, and *mythology*? What was most surprising to you? Why?
2. Why do you think the Holy Spirit moved on both Peter and Jude to write about the fallen angel incident? What is the significance of this event being mentioned in the New Testament?
3. Jesus Himself said, "As it was in the days of Noah, so it will be at the coming of the Son of Man" (Matthew 24:37 *NIV*). Stop and think about what took place in the days of Noah and what the world was like (*see* Genesis 6:1-13). What things might we experience again just before Jesus returns for us?

LESSON 2

TOPIC

People of the Old Testament

SYNOPSIS

There are some truly extraordinary individuals that appear on the pages of the Old Testament. People like Noah, who built the legendary ark that survived the Great Deluge, and Abraham the father of faith through whom all the people of the earth are blessed, are great examples. And yet even people like Noah and Abraham who had great victories, also had real personal failures.

Although we might think it would be better to omit from Scripture the low points in these people's lives, God chose to leave them in. By doing so He lets us know that there is no such thing as a perfect person, and just as the great heroes of old had low moments, so will we. But God can take our messes and turn them into a message that will help others — if we let Him.

The emphasis of this lesson:

In this lesson, you'll discover nine examples of the rapture in Scripture. You'll also learn some not-so-well-known facts about the character of Noah, Abraham, and Lot. There are lessons we can learn from the honorable as well as the dishonorable aspects of their lives.

Nine Examples of the Rapture Mentioned in Scripture

Many people today — including many Christians — wonder if the rapture of the Church is real. Some skeptics say, "Oh, the idea that God is somehow going to catch people away and transport them into another realm is just a fairy tale." But that is simply not true. The rapture is not a new idea. According to Scripture, God has been catching people away since the very beginning of time.

Enoch

The first rapture ever recorded in Scripture is in Genesis 5:24, which says, "And Enoch walked with God: and he was not; for God took him." The Amplified version of this verse says, "And Enoch walked [in habitual fellowship] with God; and he was not, for God took him [home with Him]." Enoch was so intimately close with God, God couldn't stand to be separated from him, so He raptured Enoch.

Elijah

Enoch was not the only person that the Bible mentions was raptured. There are many others. In Second Kings 2:11, it says, "And it came to pass, as they still went on, and talked, that, behold, there appeared a chariot of fire, and horses of fire, and parted them both asunder; and Elijah went up by a whirlwind into heaven." Elijah was "raptured" into heaven in a chariot of fire. This is the second rapture described in Scripture.

Isaiah

In addition to Enoch and Elijah, the prophet Isaiah was also temporarily *caught up* into Heaven. The Bible says, "In the year that king Uzziah died I saw also the Lord sitting upon a throne, high and lifted up, and his train filled the temple" (Isaiah 6:1). Isaiah went on to describe the angels around God's throne and their activity in Heaven. After an angel purified his mouth with a coal from the altar, he then returned to earth to be God's messenger to the people of Israel.

Philip

Looking at Acts Chapter 8, we find the story of the apostle Philip ministering to the Ethiopian official on the road to Gaza. The Bible says, "Then Philip opened his mouth, and began at the same scripture, and preached unto him Jesus" (Acts 8:35). After Philip finished sharing the Gospel, he baptized the Ethiopian in a roadside river. "And when they were come up out of the water, the Spirit of the Lord *caught away* Philip, that the eunuch saw him no more: and he went on his way rejoicing. But Philip was found at Azotus..." (Acts 8:39,40). Like a scene from a science fiction movie, Philip was suddenly "caught away" by the Spirit of the Lord and transported a few miles away to another town. Interestingly, the phrase "caught away" in Greek is the same word for "caught up" in First Thessalonians 4:17, which describes the rapture of the Church.

Paul

In Paul's second letter to the believers at Corinth, He described a rapture that he himself experienced. He said, "I know a man in Christ who fourteen years ago — whether in the body I do not know, or whether out of the body I do not know, God knows — such a one was caught up to the third heaven...How he was caught up into Paradise and heard inexpressible words, which it is not lawful for a man to utter" (2 Corinthians 12:2,4 *NKJV*). Like Isaiah, Paul was temporarily raptured into Heaven, and God revealed things to him that Paul could not put into words.

John

The apostle John had a similar experience. After being imprisoned on the Isle of Patmos for his bold faith, John received the Revelation of Jesus Christ — from Christ Himself! During this supernatural download, John said, "...I looked, and, behold, a door was opened in heaven: and the first voice which I heard was as it were of a trumpet talking with me; which said, Come up hither, and I will shew thee things which must be hereafter" (Revelation 4:1). Here we see John was transported, or raptured, into the presence of the Lord.

The Two End-Time Witnesses

There is another rapture recorded in the book of Revelation, and it involves the two end-time witnesses. Jesus said for three and a half years, these two witnesses will prophesy and preach the Gospel, and no one will be able to touch them. When they are finished with their assignment, the beast out of the bottomless pit will kill them. But after three and a half days, they will be raised to life again by the Spirit of God.

In that moment, the Bible says these two witnesses will hear "...a great voice from heaven saying unto them, Come up hither. And they ascended up to heaven in a cloud; and their enemies beheld them" (Revelation 11:12). Jesus' two witnesses during the great tribulation will be raptured into the presence of the Lord while the whole world watches.

Jesus

When Jesus had finished His work on earth, He told His disciples to wait in the city of Jerusalem until they were clothed with the power of the Holy Spirit (*see* Acts 1:4,5,8). The Bible says, "And when he had spoken these things, while they beheld, he was taken up; and a cloud received him out of their sight" (Acts 1:9). Jesus Himself was taken up into the heavens. Once again, we see a picture of the rapture.

The Church

One day soon, another rapture is going to take place — the rapture of the Church! God gave the apostle Paul a clear revelation of this glorious event, and he wrote about it in First Thessalonians 4:16 and 17: "For the Lord himself shall descend from heaven with a shout, with the voice of the archangel, and with the trump of God: and the dead in Christ shall rise first: Then we which are alive and remain shall be caught up together with them in the clouds, to meet the Lord in the air: and so shall we ever be with the Lord."

Friend, one of these days, Jesus is going to descend into the lower atmosphere, and when He does, He's going to give a commanding shout that galvanizes all the troops of Heaven and His Church on earth. Instantly, the dead in Christ are going to be raised to new life and provided incorruptible bodies. Then the remnant of believers who are alive and awaiting His return will be snatched out of harm's way and caught up to meet the Lord in the air! This is the greatest rapture of all raptures, and it is going to take place soon!

(For an in-depth look at the rapture of the Church, check out Rick's teaching series called *The Coming of the Antichrist*. It will help you know and understand what the Bible says about Christ's return.)

What Kind of Man Was Noah?

Have you ever really sat down and thought about Noah? *What kind of man was he? Was he smart? Was he rich? And just how long did it take him to build the ark?* Although the Bible doesn't give a ton of details about him, we can come to some logical conclusions regarding his character and his efforts.

Usually when people think of Noah and the ark, they imagine a small, overloaded toy boat like those pictured in children's books. Likewise, they imagine Noah and his three sons with small hammers and handsaws laboring alone to construct the ship, but that was probably not the case. Building the ark to God's specifications was a massive undertaking. Think about it: God said make the ark 300 cubits long, 50 cubits wide, and 30 cubits high. Since a cubit was about 18-21 inches in length, this vessel was to be 450-500 feet long by 75-85 feet wide by 45-52 feet high — and have three different levels. To tackle a task of this magnitude, Noah had to have engineering capabilities.

Although it is not written in Scripture, it's likely that Noah reached out into the community and hired men to help with the project. It is also possible he organized these men into crews — one to cut down the massive amount of wood, one to transport it to the job site, and one to prepare the raw timbers and put them into place. Thus, Noah had to have good organizational and managerial skills to oversee such a project. But that's not all. He also had to have an architectural eye to develop feeding systems and sewage systems to take care of all the animals that were on the ark.

In addition to being intellectually brilliant, Noah must have also been considerably wealthy. The ark required an unprecedented amount of resources and manpower to construct, and the length of time it took to build it made the project even more costly. The first time Noah is mentioned, he was 500 years of age and he had three sons — Shem, Ham, and Japheth (*see* Genesis 5:32). When the flood finally came on the earth, the Bible says he was 600 years old (*see* Genesis 7:6). Hence, we understand from Scripture that it took about 100 years to build the ark.

Then there was the gathering of food for Noah and his family, not to mention the food to feed all the animals that would be on board. And how about those animals? The Bible says God caused the animals to come to Noah (*see* Genesis 6:20), but he and his team needed to organize them and place them into their compartments. Clearly, this project had to be carried out by a man of great wisdom, wealth, patience, and persistence. Noah was that man. He had proven himself faithful in God's eyes and he received God's favor. With the blessing of God on his life and his efforts, Noah succeeded.

Who Was the First Drunk in the Bible?

Of course no man is perfect, including Noah. If you have ever wondered who the first drunk in the Bible was, the answer is *Noah*. After being cooped up in the ark for 375 days, Noah and his family and all the animals finally exited the ship. The Bible says, "And Noah began to be a farmer, and he planted a vineyard. Then he drank of the wine and was drunk, and became uncovered in his tent" (Genesis 9:20,21 *NKJV*).

After walking in focused obedience for about a hundred years, building the ark and making it through the catastrophic flood, Noah fell off the wagon and got drunk. Now, before we point a finger of fault at Noah, how many times have we experienced a similar situation? We seem to be doing really well, and then out of nowhere we give into our fleshly nature and do something foolish. The truth is this is a part of the human experience. Thankfully, God is merciful and willing to forgive. If we will fess up after our sinful mess up, God will clean up our lives and help us move on.

When Noah stepped out of the ark and saw the post-flood environment, the world must have been drastically different than his previous pre-flood surroundings. Everything he had known had been wiped out. The trees, the landscape, and the soil itself were no longer the same. In fact, with the water having covered the highest mountains and prevailing on the earth for months, it is very likely that when Noah disembarked the ark, he was met with a great big muddy mess. It is possible that the cataclysmic changes caused Noah to become overwhelmed or even depressed. Maybe he looked around and thought, *Really? After all the years of laborious preparation and then all the sleepless days and nights of waiting and wondering while floating on the water, this is what I've inherited? You've got to be kidding.*

What exactly went through Noah's mind, we don't know. What we do know is that he hit a low moment in his life, and he got drunk. Nevertheless, God loved him and extended His grace to Noah. In God's mind, Noah was still a hero. In fact, he was so legendary that God moved on the heart of the writer of Hebrews to include Noah in the "hall of faith" heroes listed in Hebrews 11. Aren't you glad that God still loves you in your low moments? Isn't it an encouragement to know that even when you make wrong choices, you are not disqualified? Through faith in Christ's finished work of redemption, you have forgiveness of sin and full restoration. In Christ, *you* are also a hero of faith!

Why Did Nimrod Build the Tower of Babel?

Immediately following the story of Noah and the Flood, the Bible records what has been referred to as the Table of the Nations in Genesis chapter 10. In detail, we learn of the descendants from each of Noah's sons — Shem, Ham, and Japheth. In these verses, we get a close look at the lineage of Ham and see that his sons were Cush, Mizraim, Phut, and Canaan; from Cush came the infamous leader named Nimrod (*see* Genesis 10:6-8). The Bible says, "He was a mighty hunter before the Lord…And the beginning of his kingdom was Babel, and Erech, and Accad, and Calneh, in the Land of Shinar" (Genesis 10:9,10).

This brings us to the story of the Tower of Babel in Genesis chapter 11. There are many powerful principles packed into this narrative nestled in Genesis 11, but the one question that people often ask about this event is, *why did Nimrod build the tower?* Although the Bible doesn't say much about Nimrod's motives, it does give us some insight in Genesis 11:4: "And they said, Go to, let us build us a city and a tower, whose top may reach unto heaven; and let us make us a name, lest we be scattered abroad upon the face of the whole earth."

Within this verse, we can see a component of *pride*: "Let us make us a name." We can also discern an element of *rebellion* and possibly *fear*. After the Flood, God had told the people to be fruitful, multiply, and replenish the earth (*see* Genesis 9:7). The people's decision to build a tower and avoid being scattered across the face of the earth was in rebellion to God's instructions.

There is another reason for Nimrod's actions — one that is not recorded in Scripture, but was handed down by the ancient rabbis and communicated to the rabbinical scribes to write down. They said that Nimrod remembered the destructive details of the Flood, and he never wanted to suffer again like the rest of the earth had suffered. Therefore, Nimrod wanted to build a tower tall enough that if God ever sent another worldwide flood, he could escape it by going to the top of the tower. Although this is not a biblical answer, it is a brilliant possibility nonetheless.

Who Was the Most Famous Moon Worshiper in the Old Testament?

You may have heard Abraham called the Father of Faith, but what you may not know is that before he put his faith in the One True God, Abraham was a worshiper of the moon. The Bible says that Abraham was from Ur of the Chaldees, and in Ur of the Chaldees, they worshiped the crescent moon. And as part of their religious ceremonies, they offered their babies as sacrifices to the moon.

What is very interesting is that if you look at most of the Muslim flags from around the world, they have the symbol of the crescent moon. For years, Rick has worked with a highly educated Muslim tour guide from the country of Turkey, and he once told Rick, "The crescent moon that we Muslims use on our flags and on all of our emblems comes from the ancient pagan religion that was practiced in Ur of the Chaldees."

History confirms that those who lived in the Mesopotamian city of Ur were worshipers of the moon, which would have included Abraham *before* he met God. But then something glorious happened. Stephen described the event when he stood up and preached to the Jewish leaders in Acts 7:2. He said, "…Men, brethren, and fathers, hearken; The God of glory appeared unto our father Abraham, when he was in Mesopotamia, before he dwelt in Haran."

Abraham was not expecting an encounter with God, but suddenly he found himself literally surrounded by a cloud of His glory. That is what this verse of Scripture says in the Greek. The Bible tells us that God took him by surprise, and that on that day He "…preached the gospel to Abraham beforehand, saying, 'In you all the nations shall be blessed" (Galatians 3:8 *NKJV*). Deeply moved in his heart, Abraham abandoned his worship of the moon, and his involvement in paganism and the occult ceased. From that moment on he began his lifelong journey of following God's voice.

What Character in the Old Testament Married His Sister?

In the ancient past, when men and women entered into marriage, it was not uncommon for siblings to marry. However, it seems that sometime between the Great Flood and the time of Moses, a genetic problem developed in the offspring of close relatives. When God gave Israel the Law through Moses, He included a commandment for no one to marry a close relation (*see* Leviticus 18).

Abraham lived approximately 500 years before Moses, and he did marry his half-sister Sarah, the daughter of his father but not his mother (*see* Genesis 20:12). On two occasions during his travels in Canaan and the surrounding countries, he asked his wife, Sarah, to tell anyone who asked that she was his sister. He did this when he went into Egypt because of a famine in Canaan (*see* Genesis 12:10-20); and he did it again when he went into the country of Gerar (*see* Genesis 20:1-13).

Although it was true that Sarah was Abraham's half-sister, she was first and foremost his wife. Thus, Abraham, the Father of Faith, told a half-truth (which is a whole lie). Fear motivated him to lie, and then he asked his wife to lie. He was afraid that the foreigners would kill him in order to take Sarah. This lets us know that none of us — not even the Father of Faith — always walks in perfection.

Was Lot Gay?

Abraham's nephew Lot was living in the wicked city of Sodom, which was near Gomorrah, for many years. And while the environment was certainly dominated by a spirit of homosexuality, nowhere in Scripture does it indicate that Lot himself was a homosexual. What we do know is that little by little, Lot became more and more intertwined with the people of Sodom. The Bible says that initially Lot "pitched his tent toward Sodom" (*see* Genesis 13:12). But eventually, he moved inside the city and became one of its leaders.

When the two angels arrived at the city gates of Sodom, Lot was sitting at the gate (*see* Genesis 19:1). In those days, city officials took their seat at the city gates, which was where the business of the city took place. Although we don't know exactly what his official title was, we do know he was a prominent leader in Sodom and that he had received the endorsement of the city. Otherwise, they would not have let him sit at the gate.

Don't miss this point. The exceedingly wicked city of Sodom approved of Lot. They saw him as one of them. In fact, he was so intertwined in the lives of the Sodomites that when the men of the city came to his house and demanded to have sex with the two angels, Lot called them *brothers*. The Bible says, "And they called unto Lot, and said unto him, Where are the men which came in to thee this night? Bring them out unto us, that we may know them. And Lot went out at the door unto them, and shut the door after him, and said, I pray you, brethren, do not so wickedly" (Genesis 19:5-7).

There Lot stood on the porch of his house, speaking to all Sodomites and calling them *brethren*. This shows how connected he had become to the people of Sodom. He had so defiled himself mentally, emotionally, and spiritually that his soul had been worn down and calloused by their perverted ways. In the process, he had ruined his reputation.

Yet, in spite of how morally messed up he was, God called him a *righteous* man. The Bible says, "And [God] delivered just Lot, vexed with the filthy conversation of the wicked: (For that righteous man dwelling among them, in seeing and hearing, vexed his righteous soul from day to day with their unlawful deeds)" (2 Peter 2:7,8). Twice in one verse, the apostle Peter tells us Lot was a righteous man. Even though he was not living very righteously, God declared him righteous. Therefore, we do not believe that Lot was gay.

What's very interesting about Lot's story is that he was living in a city that was moments away from being utterly destroyed by God, but he was clueless. Abraham, on the other hand, lived in relationship with God and was informed beforehand of what was about to happen. In fact, it was Abraham's prayers that saved Lot from being killed. The Bible says, "… When God destroyed the cities of the plain, that *God remembered Abraham*, and sent Lot out of the midst of the overthrow…" (Genesis 19:29).

Friend, that is how powerful your prayers are! If you know a Christian that has wandered from their faith, don't just wash your hands and say, "There's no hope for them." Take the position of Abraham — pray for them. God will respond to your prayers just like he responded to the prayers of Abraham, and He will deliver that Christian for your sake. God will move in that person's life because *you* prayed.

STUDY QUESTIONS

Study to shew thyself approved unto God, a workman that needeth
not to be ashamed, rightly dividing the word of truth.
— 2 Timothy 2:15

1. Of the nine examples of the rapture mentioned in Scripture, which ones have you *not* heard of? What is most intriguing to you about these examples? How do they strengthen your belief in the coming rapture of the Church?

2. When you read the details of God speaking to Noah and instructing him on how to build the ark and prepare for the flood (*see* Genesis 6:8-22), what stands out most about his character? Imagine *you* are Noah, and God has just given the ark project to you. How do you think you would handle it? What do you think would be your greatest challenge?

3. Again, imagine *you* are Noah, and you're getting off the ark and seeing the post-flood world for the first time. Everything that you remember has been wiped out, and you're starting all over again. How do you think you would react? What do you think would be your greatest challenge? (Consider Genesis 9:1-21 as you answer.)

PRACTICAL APPLICATION

But be ye doers of the word, and not hearers only,
deceiving your own selves.
— James 1:22

1. Why do you think God chose to include in Scripture many of the faults and failures of the heroes of faith? How does seeing their shortcomings help you in your personal walk with God?

2. The Bible says that one of the ways we overcome the enemy is by sharing "the word of our testimony" (*see* Revelation 12:11). What aspects of your testimony (especially your mistakes) have you been able to share with others that has really helped bring them freedom? Who have you been able to share it with?

3. Aren't you glad that God still loves you in your low moments? Isn't it an encouragement to know that even when you make wrong choices, you are not disqualified? Why not take a few moments to sincerely

thank God for His mercy, patience, and forgiveness. He is worthy to be praised!

TOPIC

Answers From the Old Testament

SYNOPSIS

For many years, long before the invention of radio or television, there was in the center of every Russian home what is called a *samovar*. It is the ancient equivalent of a hot-water tea kettle with a tiny built-in chimney to heat up the water. People would insert wood chips, pinecones, or small lumps of coal and set it on fire. Once the water was piping hot, tea or other hot beverages were made and then served through the spout.

The Russian samovar became a cultural emblem of hospitality. People would gather around it and enjoy hours of fellowship — telling stories, imparting humor, and sharing personal experiences. Rick has a Russian samovar on his television set as a reminder of the fellowship we share as we sit around the Word of God and hear powerful stories of truth. As you begin this lesson, open your heart to the truth of God's Word and the work of the Holy Spirit in your life.

The emphasis of this lesson:

In this lesson, you'll witness the incredible faith of Isaac as he was about to be sacrificed by his father; the proof of David's confidence in the Lord to defeat Goliath; and who had the most dysfunctional marriage in the Old Testament. You'll also learn the true identities of the legendary sorcerers that stood against Moses, if Balaam was a prophet of God, and what Old Testament prophet served five pagan kings.

How Old Was Isaac When Abraham Offered Him As a Sacrifice at Mount Moriah?

Probably the greatest test in Abraham's life came when God asked him to sacrifice his only son, Isaac, on Mount Moriah. We read about this event in Genesis 22. Have you ever wondered how old Isaac was when this took place? Many people have had this question.

Although most people envision him as a young boy between 8 to 12 years old — or even a young teenager — he was actually much older. According to the Jewish historian Josephus, Isaac was 25 years old when this event took place, which means Abraham would have been 125 years old. If you do the math chronologically that's how old they would be.

Knowing that Isaac was about 25 years of age places this story in a whole new light. Actually, it says a great deal about Isaac because it means he was a strapping young man in his prime. At the age of 25, he didn't have to obey his father. He could have argued or fought with Abraham about being sacrificed, but he didn't. Instead, Isaac showed honor, humility, and tremendous submission to authority.

When Abraham bound Isaac and placed him on the altar, he was cooperative, which means Abraham was not the only one who was walking in faith. He had successfully taught his son to walk in faith as well. Isaac trusted his dad and believed that if God had asked for him to be sacrificed, he was willing to do his part. Just as Abraham was believing for a resurrection, so was Isaac. This story powerfully demonstrates the influence of a godly father. You too can have the same kind of influence on your children and grandchildren by choosing to walk in relationship with God daily.

Who Had the Most Dysfunctional Marriage in the Old Testament?

Now while Abraham certainly did many things well, there are some areas of his life where he struggled. If you've ever wondered who had the most dysfunctional marriage in the Old Testament, the answer would likely be Abraham and Sarah. This fact is made most clear at the end of Sarah's life. According to Genesis 22:19, after Abraham and Isaac returned from Mount Moriah, "...They rose up and went together to Beersheba; and Abraham dwelt at Beersheba."

Where was Sarah while Abraham was living in Beersheba? Genesis 23:1 and 2 says, "And Sarah was an hundred and seven and twenty years old: these were the years of the life of Sarah. And Sarah died in Kirjatharba; the same is Hebron in the land of Canaan: and Abraham came to mourn for Sarah, and to weep for her."

Did you catch that? Abraham was *not* with Sarah when she died. They were living in different cities. What happened that caused them to have separate living arrangements, the Bible does not say. Nevertheless, something took place that resulted in them living apart. This tells us that Abraham and Sarah — the "Father and Mother of Faith" — were not perfect. Yes, they did many things right, but a healthy marriage they did not model.

In fact, the Bible says Sarah had to learn how to call Abraham "lord" (*see* 1 Peter 3:6). We know from Scripture that Abraham made many mistakes in his walk of faith, which probably made it very difficult at times to follow him. Likewise, there were probably occasions when Sarah was very difficult to lead. They were both strong-willed individuals. And when you come to the very end of their lives, they were not even living together.

What is interesting is that by the time we cross over into the New Testament and we read about Abraham, his mistakes are not discussed. The grace of God covers his poor choices, and the only things God prompts the writers to describe are what he did right. That's the power of the blood of Jesus! Once our sin is confessed and under the Blood, what we did wrong is no longer discussed! The Bible says, "As far as the east is from the west, so far hath he removed our transgressions from us" (Psalm 103:12).

Why Did David Choose Five Smooth Stones When He Went Out To Fight Goliath?

First Samuel 17:40 tells us that as David was going out to fight Goliath, "...He took his staff in his hand, and chose him five smooth stones out of the brook, and put them in a shepherd's bag which he had, even in a scrip; and his sling was in his hand: and he drew near to the Philistine." This verse has raised the question among many believers: *Why five stones?*

The answer to this question is found in Second Samuel 21:18-22, which tells us that Goliath had four sons, and they were also giants. This indicates that when David went out to fight Goliath, he only took one stone to hit Goliath and one stone to hit each of his sons if they chose to come out after him. Thus, David was so confident that God was with him, he believed he would take down each giant with one stone each.

What Were the Names of the Sorcerers That Moses Confronted?

When we read the account of the nation of Israel being delivered from slavery in Egypt, there are two magicians or sorcerers who repeatedly stood against Moses and were able to duplicate virtually every plague God had brought on the land of Egypt. Although the book of Exodus doesn't give us their names, their identity is recorded elsewhere. For example, the apostle Paul identified them in Second Timothy 3:8 "…as Jannes and Jambres [who] withstood Moses…."

How did he know that information? Because living in Egypt in the First and Second Century BC was the largest group of Jews outside of the land of Israel. These weren't just any Jews; these were the greatest theologians among the Jews anywhere in the world. In fact, these Alexandrian Jews were such a part of the intelligentsia of the region that they were highly revered for their knowledge. It was these Jewish scholars in Alexandria, Egypt who were drafted to translate the Old Testament Hebrew Scriptures into Greek. Seventy of the brightest of the bright came together to create what we have come to know as the *Septuagint* — the very Bible that Jesus quoted from during His ministry.

Furthermore, the city of Alexandria, Egypt became home to the world-renowned library of Alexandria. This was a repository of the best knowledge and information in the entire ancient world at that time. Interestingly, the legendary sorcerers Jannes and Jambres who withstood Moses were so renowned that their names were recorded in that library. They were also documented in other secular writings from there in Egypt, all the way to Greece and Rome.

What Was the First Case of Incest Recorded in the Bible?

Sexual sin is not something new to our generation. It has been around since just after the fall of man. Some have said that when Noah lay drunk inside of his tent and his son Ham came in, Ham did something sexually perverted to him. But because we don't really know that for sure, it appears that the earliest recorded case of incest in Scripture is that of Lot and his two daughters.

After Lot was delivered from the destruction of Sodom where he and his family had been living, he ended up dwelling in a cave with only his two daughters. If you remember, as the family was escaping for their lives, Lot's wife turned back and looked at the city, and she became a pillar of salt. From the vantage point of their cave in Zoar, Lot and his daughters saw nothing left to the civilization they once knew. It was as if the entire earth had been destroyed. It seems to have looked the same way to Abraham when he got up the next morning (*see* Genesis 19:27,28).

When Lot's girls looked out and saw Sodom and all the cities of the plain obliterated, they thought they were the last of the human race. In that moment, the Bible says, "...The firstborn said unto the younger, Our father is old, and there is not a man in the earth to come in unto us after the manner of all the earth (Genesis 19:31). When we read the rest of the story in Genesis 19, we see that to preserve Lot's seed, they got him drunk two nights in a row, and each daughter slept with their father and conceived a child. This was the first real documented case of incest in Scripture.

Was Balaam a Prophet or a Witch?

Many Christians get confused about Balaam, believing that he was a prophet of God that was backslidden, but that was not the case. Rick highlights valuable information on Balaam in his book *No Room for Compromise: Christ's Message to Today's Church.*

The bulk of what is known about Balaam outside of the Old Testament comes from the ancient Jewish community, especially those written by Jewish scholars in the city of Alexandria. Alexandrian Jews were highly educated and renowned for their ability to keep detailed, historical records. And from the commentaries written by these Jewish historians we know a lot about Balaam. Perhaps the most telling is what was written by Philo. As one of the leading Jewish intellectuals in the city of Alexandria, he said that Balaam was a man renowned above all men for his skill as a *diviner*. Now, a diviner is not a prophet of God. A diviner is one involved in occult activity.

The city of Alexandria was a long-time center of Egyptian witchcraft, sorcery, wizardry, incantations, enchantments, magic, and spells, and the educated Jewish scholars from that city were familiar with these practices and their descriptions. They had seen occult practices during their sojourn in Egypt, and they knew the difference between a prophet of God and a sorcerer. For them to write that Balaam was renowned above all men for his skill as a diviner, indicates Balaam was a witch.

Possibly the most famous Jewish scholar was Josephus, and he wrote that Balaam was among the greatest of the prophets at that time. Josephus' use of the word "prophet" is where people get confused. When they hear the word "prophet," they think he must have been a prophet of God. But that is a mistake. There were all kinds of prophets — some godly and some ungodly. For example, if you went to the city of Delphi in Greece in ancient times, there was a person there known as the Oracle of Delphi. Although many called her a prophetess, she was totally immersed in the occult.

To be clear, the word "prophet" or "prophetess" merely described *a person who was a voice piece for the spirit-realm.* There were prophets of God, and there were pagan prophets. So when Josephus said that Balaam was a prophet, it doesn't mean that he was a prophet of God. It simply means he was a voice, or mouth piece, for the spirit-realm. The use of the word "prophet" in the writings of Philo and Josephus should not be misunderstood. It does not refer to a spokesman of God, such as Moses or Elijah. Balaam and his practices were diametrically opposed to God's prohibitions regarding activities of the occult. Philo and Josephus used the word "prophet" in a general sense to denote *one who was able to foresee the future.*

The Bible clearly states that Balaam was a diviner who operated with the powers of divination, which is witchcraft (*see* Numbers 24:1). Other common names for diviners include a foretelling seer, a soothsayer, a consulter of familiar spirits, an enchanter, a necromancer, a wizard, a witch, or an instrument through whom the spirit-realm speaks, like a medium or a clairvoyant.

What is interesting is that the Alexandrian Jews wrote that Balaam and Moses lived at the same time. Moreover, they said that just as Moses was God's main prophet, Balaam was the legendary prophet in the pagan world. As a matter of fact, Balaam was so well-known and sought after that Balak, the leader of Moab, sent an envoy of royal princes to him, offering him indescribable riches to coax him into making the long journey to come and curse the Israelites.

If you read the entire story of Balaam, it says he kept trying to curse the people of God, but he couldn't do it. He kept going from mountaintop to mountaintop where he would make a sacrifice by killing an animal and then try to foretell the future. Many people who don't understand how pagan prophets operated think that he was sacrificing to God, but he wasn't.

As a pagan prophet — or diviner — Balaam used a variety of occult practices to foresee the future like many other ancient diviners did. But one especially common practice was to slaughter an animal and spread it's entrails on an altar in an attempt to read the future by analyzing the strewn organs. Numbers 23 tells us Balak took Balaam to multiple mountain tops, giving Balaam multiple vantage points to see the Israelites and curse them. Each time, Balaam offered up animal sacrifices before he tried to curse Israel. He was performing this common act of divination, but it gave him no power to be able to curse the people of God.

In fact, Balaam himself said, "Surely there is no enchantment against Jacob, neither is there any divination against Israel…" (Numbers 23:23). In other words, no form of sorcery or wizardry would work against the people of God. When you put all of this together, it becomes clear that Balaam was not a prophet of God; he was a pagan prophet.

When we come to Numbers Chapter 31, we see that God spoke to Moses and told him to send the Israelite army against the Midianites. Moses obeyed, and Israel was victorious. Amongst the casualties of the battle, was the infamous pagan prophet Balaam. He had been killed with the sword, bringing his divination days to an end (*see* Numbers 31:8; Joshua 13:22).

What Old Testament Prophet Served Five Pagan Kings?

There is a very interesting fact about the prophet Daniel that is not widely known. What is it you ask? Daniel served five different pagan kings over the course of his lifetime. During his teenage years, he was taken into Babylonian captivity, along with his three close friends — Shadrach, Meshach, and Abednego. He served as a high-ranking advisor to each king all the way up into his nineties.

One of the most encouraging aspects of Daniel's life is his longevity. It is a powerful reminder — especially for older believers — that God is never finished with us just because we're up in age. In fact, this truth sheds a whole new light on the concept of retirement. The truth is, you can search the Bible from Genesis to Revelation, and you will not find the idea of retirement anywhere. The concept is relatively new and began about a hundred years ago.

When people retire, they begin to die. It is not healthy. Studies show that people without purpose begin to shut down faster than those who are active. God never puts His children on the shelf because they get older. On the contrary, when a believer gets older, they are more beneficial than ever before. Think about it: If you are an older believer, you have walked through countless experiences and finally have priceless knowledge that others can benefit from. So if you are older, don't let anyone younger discount you because of your age. They need your voice! You have something to say!

STUDY QUESTIONS

Study to shew thyself approved unto God, a workman that needeth not to be ashamed, rightly dividing the word of truth.
— 2 Timothy 2:15

1. In the last two lessons, we have looked at many details about Abraham's life — some good and some not-so-good. Of all that you know about Abraham and Sarah, what is the most encouraging example from their lives? What about this gives you hope?

2. Lot was living in a place that was moments away from being utterly destroyed by God, yet he was totally clueless of what was about to happen. Abraham, on the other hand, lived in relationship with God and was informed *beforehand* of what was going to happen. How do Amos 3:7; First Corinthians 2:9,10; John 16:12,13; and Psalm 25:14 confirm that this type of foreknowledge is available to you?

3. One of the most disturbing stories in Scripture is when Lot's daughters commit incest with him to preserve their family line. According to Genesis 19:36-38, what were the names of the children birthed out of this perverted union? What do you know about the nations these children founded? What does this end result of Lot's choices speak to you personally?

4. Prior to this lesson, what did you know about Balaam? Did you understand him to be a prophet of God? According to Numbers 22:21-35, what extremely bizarre event happened to him while he was

on his way to meet Balak? How has this lesson expanded your understanding of who Balaam was?

PRACTICAL APPLICATION

> But be ye doers of the word, and not hearers only,
> deceiving your own selves.
> —James 1:22

1. According to the Jewish historian Josephus, Isaac was 25 years old
   and Abraham was 125 when God asked Abraham to sacrifice Isaac on
   Mount Moriah. How does this fact change the way you see this story
   — including your view of Isaac?
2. The Bible says, "...When God destroyed the cities of the plain, that
   God remembered Abraham, and sent Lot out of the midst of the
   overthrow..." (Genesis 19:29). It was Abraham's prayers that saved
   Lot from being killed.

   • Who do you know like Lot that once was in close fellowship with
     God, but over time has compromised their beliefs and become
     entangled and defiled by the world's system?

   • Are you praying and interceding for them? If you haven't been
     praying for them, why not take the position of Abraham and begin
     to pray for God's mercy on their life and that their eyes would be
     opened to the truth. Like Abraham, your prayers make an eternal
     difference (*see* James 5:16).

LESSON 4

TOPIC

Angels and Monsters

SYNOPSIS

If you have ever watched the Renner TV program, you may have noticed
a beautiful black-lacquered box on the set. It is an exquisite, hand-painted
black box from a little village called Fedoskino. Artists first began creating

these decorative keepsakes in 1795. The one on Rick's set was given to the ministry as a gift.

The significance of this miniature box is found in the intricate picture that is painted on its cover. It is a magnificent illustration of a fight of faith. The scene depicts Peter the Great standing for truth while other people are beginning to depart from the faith and theologians are debating what faith actually is. This Fedoskino black-lacquered box is a powerful reminder of the words of Jude 3, which says, "...Earnestly contend for the faith which was once delivered unto the saints."

Friend, we have a God-given responsibility to guard and contend for the faith, which means to spiritually fight to keep the Christian faith in its purest form. One of the best ways to do that is to dig deep into the pages of Scripture and understand what it is saying. That is the reason for this Question and Answer series with Rick Renner.

The emphasis of this lesson:

Who was the naked boy in the Garden of Gethsemane? How old was Jesus when the Magi arrived to worship Him? And does the New Testament talk about monsters and UFO's? Rick answers these questions and more in this fourth lesson on angels and monsters.

Who Was the Naked Boy in the Garden of Gethsemane?

Did you know that the Bible talks about a naked boy that was in the Garden of Gethsemane the night Jesus was betrayed and arrested? Mark 14:51 and 52 describes something that took place that was quite out of the ordinary. It says, "And there followed him a certain young man, having a linen cloth cast about his naked body; and the young men laid hold on him: and he left the linen cloth, and fled from them naked."

A number of scholars have explained that the young man who was naked in Gethsemane was John Mark himself. They claim that for some unknown reason, he suddenly appeared in the garden without any clothes, but that makes no sense and doesn't fit within the context of the passage. Still others have stated that the naked young man was the apostle John. They speculate that when Jesus was being arrested, John tried to create a diversion by removing his clothes to distract the soldiers. This, too, is an outlandish idea that doesn't fit within the narrative of what took place.

To know the true identity of the naked boy in Gethsemane that night, we must understand the original Greek used in this passage as well as the history of the garden itself. During the First Century, the Garden of Gethsemane not only contained an olive orchard and multiple caves, but also an ancient cemetery at its base. This means that there were many graves in the garden — primarily for wealthy people — and a number of them would have been freshly dug for those who had just been buried.

It was customary for Jews to bury their dead naked. Prior to burial, the body of the deceased was ceremonially cleansed and purified. The naked corpse was then carefully wrapped with a "linen cloth," which is the phrase we see appearing twice in Mark 14:51 and 52. It is the Greek word *sindon*, which is the New Testament word that *depicts a linen cloth in which individuals were wrapped for burial*. Thus, it was *a burial shroud used for covering a dead body in the grave*. It is the exact word used to describe Jesus' burial shroud in Matthew 27:59; Mark 15:46; and Luke 23:53.

The night that Jesus was arrested, the Bible says, "Judas then, having received a band of men and officers from the chief priests and Pharisees, cometh thither with lanterns and torches and weapons" (John 18:3). The phrase "band of men" is the Greek word *speira*, and it describes *a military cohort*, which is *a tenth of a legion*, or *approximately 600 well-trained and equipped soldiers*. The fact that Judas came with hundreds of well-armed soldiers to arrest Jesus indicates that he was well aware of Jesus' supernatural power and had told the Jewish leaders about it. Hence, they approved the dispatch of 600 soldiers.

The Bible says when this armed mob found Jesus, He looked at them and said, "…Whom seek ye? They answered him, Jesus of Nazareth. Jesus saith unto them, I am he…" (John 18:4,5). In Greek, the words "I am" is the phrase *Ego eimi*, which means, *"I AM!"* These are the same words God used to describe Himself to Moses in Exodus 3:14. By using these words, Jesus was declaring that He was — and is — *God in the flesh*!

Scripture goes on to say, "As soon then as he had said unto them, I am he, they went backward, and fell to the ground" (John 18:6). In Greek, "went backward" means the soldiers *staggered and stumbled backward, as if some force had hit them and was pushing them back and down*. The word "fell" is the Greek word *pipto*, which means *to fall* and depicts *a person who falls so hard that it appears he has fallen dead or has fallen like a corpse.* When Jesus said "I AM!" a divine blast of power was discharged that knocked hundreds of soldiers flat to the ground.

Apparently, that same supernatural blast of power released through Jesus' words also resurrected a young man that had recently died and been buried! When Jesus answered the soldiers and said "I AM!" power touched this young man, and he came crawling out of his tomb. He had no idea of the events that were unfolding in the Garden of Gethsemane. When some of the soldiers who were arresting Jesus saw this naked boy, they immediately tried to grab him. The last thing they wanted was the news of another resurrection. But with quick agility, the young man escaped naked, leaving the "linen cloth" or burial shroud in their hands.

Therefore, the naked boy in the Garden of Gethsemane was a young man who had been raised from the dead. This was peripheral resurrection; it was not intentional. The power released through Jesus was just that strong!

How Old Was Jesus When the Magi Arrived To Worship Him?

The traditional picture of the nativity scene we see on greeting cards and in movies today is actually quite different than what took place the night Jesus was born. Of course Mary, Joseph, and Jesus were there, and the Bethlehem shepherds were also present. But what about the wise men? Were they there the night Jesus was born? Did they visit Him in a stable as a newborn, or did they find Him somewhere else after He was born?

The Bible says, "Now when Jesus was born in Bethlehem of Judea in the days of Herod the king, behold, there came wise men from the east to Jerusalem, saying, Where is he that is born King of the Jews? For we have seen his star in the east, and are come to worship him. And when Herod the king had heard these things, he was troubled, and all of Jerusalem with him. And when he had gathered all the chief priest and scribes of the people together, he demanded of them where Christ should be born. And they said unto him, In Bethlehem of Judea..." (Matthew 2:1-5).

Indeed, Jesus was born in Bethlehem, but not in a wooden stable as tradition often depicts. The place of His birth was a cave where animals were kept, and when the Magi saw Jesus, He was no longer in Bethlehem. Luke 2:39 confirms this, saying, "And when they [Mary and Joseph] had performed all things according to the law of the Lord, they returned into Galilee, to their own city *Nazareth*." The "things" that Mary and Joseph did while in Bethlehem were to circumcise Jesus when He was eight days old and then dedicate Him to the Lord forty days after His birth according to the completion of Mary's days of her purification (*see* Luke 2:22). Therefore, the place over which the star came and "stood" was in Nazareth, *not* Bethlehem.

Matthew 2:11 tells us what happened when the Magi arrived. It says, "And when they were come into the house, they saw the young child with Mary his mother, and fell down, and worshipped him...." Notice the word "house" in this verse. It is the Greek word *oikos*, which describes *a house*. Again, this was not the cave in Bethlehem where Jesus was born. It was a house in Nazareth. Once the forty days of Mary's purification were completed and Jesus was dedicated to God, the holy family returned to their home town in Nazareth.

When the wise men came into the house, the Bible says they saw the "young child." In Greek, this phrase is the word *paidon*, which describes *a child in training*. It is the same word Herod used in Matthew 2:8, when he told the wise men, "...Go and search diligently for the *young child*...." This word is very different than the word used to describe Jesus on the night of His birth. In Luke 2:12, the angel of the Lord called Him a "babe," which is the Greek word *brephos*, meaning *a newborn infant only a few hours old*. The use of the word *paidon* — translated here as "young child" — lets us know that Jesus was no longer an infant, but a *toddler*.

The fact is the wise men visited Jesus at His house in Nazareth about two years after His birth. He was a toddler learning how to walk and talk. It was at that time they showered the young child with lavish gifts worthy of a king and bowed low to the ground to worship Him. When they had finished worshiping Jesus and delivering their gifts, God warned them through a dream not to return to Herod, but to return home another way (*see* Matthew 2:12).

The Bible says, "Then Herod, when he saw that he was mocked of the wise men, was exceeding wroth, and sent forth, and slew all the children that were in Bethlehem..." (Matthew 2:16). Herod was still focused on Bethlehem, but Jesus was no longer there. He and His family had been living in Nazareth for two years. And just before Herod went on his murderous rampage, God had spoken to Joseph in a dream to take Jesus and Mary to

Egypt. Thus, when the enemy came in like a flood, Jesus was well out of harm's way, protected by the watchful eye of His Heavenly Father.

Rick, Have You Ever Entertained an Angel?

When you read both the Old and the New Testament, you find that sometimes angels will take on a human appearance. For example, in Genesis 18, the Bible says that three visitors came to and visited with Abraham. One was the Lord Himself, and the other two were angels that looked like people. Hence, Abraham entertained angels.

When you come to Genesis 19, these same two angels went to Sodom at night to meet with Lot, Abraham's nephew. As one of the leaders in the city, Lot was sitting at the city gate, and when he saw these visitors, he knew there was something very special about them. Apparently, they must have been very good-looking men, because the rest of the men in Sodom wanted to have sex with them (*see* Genesis 19:5). Lot brought them into his home, and they helped him and his family escape the wrath of God that came upon the city. There are stories of angels taking on a human form all through the Scriptures.

In this lesson, Rick was asked if he himself had ever entertained an angel. Here is his response in his own words:

> One time Denise and I were supposed to fly to do a meeting, and I was absolutely exhausted. I told Denise, 'I really don't want to go. I want to minister, but I have pushed myself so much lately, I just can't go any further.' As strange as it sounds, I turned to God and prayed, 'Lord, would You please do something so I can stay home this weekend?'
>
> Well, bad weather came in rather quickly, and all the flights to the city where I was scheduled to speak were canceled. The pastor from the church called me and said, 'Try to fly through Denver.' I did as he suggested, but the weather in Denver suddenly turned bad, and no one could fly through Denver.
>
> 'Try to come through Dallas,' the pastor said. But we couldn't fly through Dallas because bad weather rolled in there as well.
>
> 'Try to come through Nashville,' the pastor suggested. But when I attempted to make the arrangements, the weather suddenly became bad there too. Everywhere we tried to get a flight, the

way was blocked by inclement weather. God had heard and had answered my prayer, and I was so thankful.

Having been blessed with some much-needed downtime, I took Denise out to dinner to a local cafeteria. Once she had gotten her food, she made her way to the table. As I was standing in line to pay for our food, I began to strike up a conversation with the person standing behind me in line. Strangely, this person, whom I had never seen in my life, began to tell me all about my past and even spoke to me about my relationship with my mother.

Looking at me intently, this person said, 'You know why you're here today?'

'No,' I said. 'Why am I here?'

'This weather.... It's because of you and what you prayed.'

I stood there dumbfounded. Nobody knew what I prayed.

After paying the bill, I grabbed my food and went to the table where Denise was seated. I told her what had just happened and then added, 'Denise, is it possible that I just met the angel that brought this weather?'

Suddenly, that same person appeared standing at the table where Denise and I were sitting and began talking to us. I asked, 'Where are you from?' And without hesitation, this person responded, 'Heaven, of course' and then turned around and walked out the door.

'Denise!' I said excitedly. 'I think that was an angel!'

'I'm going to follow the angel!' Denise replied as she jumped to her feet and hurried out the door. But when she got outside, there was no one in sight.

This experience reminds me of Hebrews 13:2, which says, 'Be not forgetful to entertain strangers: for thereby some have entertained angels unawares.' Indeed, angels can take on a human appearance, and I do believe that is what Denise and I encountered that day in that cafeteria.

Does the New Testament Ever Talk About Monsters or UFOs?

In Luke 21:11, Jesus said something very intriguing. As He was giving His discourse on the Mount of Olives about events that are going to take place at the very end of the age, He said, "And great earthquakes shall be in divers places, and famines, and pestilences; and fearful sights and great signs shall there be from heaven."

The words "fearful sights" are exactly, precisely from the Greek word for *monsters*. There is no question about it. This word was classically used to describe monsters. Now, some people might say, "Well, maybe it is describing something *monstrous*." That may be true, but it is the word for *monsters*. It could be a genetic hybrid creature of some kind — or some kind of a scientific monstrous development in the end of the age. Nonetheless, the words "fearful sights" are from the Greek word for *monsters*.

In addition to "fearful sights," Jesus said, "…great signs shall there be from heaven." The word "from" here is very important, because it describes *something significant that would descend from the heavens*. Whether this is a major solar flare or a giant meteorite, it is not clear. But whatever it is, it's going to descend from the heavens. Therefore, what we can conclude from Luke 21:11 is that Jesus said *monsters* and *something significant descending from the heavens* are going to become evident in the very end of the age.

STUDY QUESTIONS

> Study to shew thyself approved unto God, a workman that needeth not to be ashamed, rightly dividing the word of truth.
> — 2 Timothy 2:15

1. The Bible actually has much to say about angels and their purpose in our lives. Take a few moments to look up these passages and identify what angels are called to do to help you on your journey of faith.
    *   Psalm 91:11,12
    *   Psalm 103:20
    *   Hebrews 1:14

2. In the story of Abraham and Lot, the Bible clearly states that angels took on the appearance of men and interacted with people. When

you hear about angels taking on a human form, what stories from Scripture come to mind? What is it about these situations that is so awe-inspiring to you? (Consider Exodus 14:19,20; Daniel 6:16-22; Luke 22:43; Acts 12:5-11.)

PRACTICAL APPLICATION

**But be ye doers of the word, and not hearers only,
deceiving your own selves.
— James 1:22**

1. Prior to this lesson, had you ever heard of the naked boy in the Garden of Gethsemane? If so, what did you know about him? How does the news of this peripheral resurrection ignite a fresh fire in your faith to believe God to move supernaturally in your own life?

2. Regarding the question of how old Jesus was when He was visited by the Magi, what new facts did you learn about this amazing moment in history? How do these insights expand your understanding of the Christmas story?

3. Rick shared an incredible story of how he and Denise encountered an angel that was literally an answer to his prayer. Have you ever entertained an angel unaware? If so, describe what took place and how the heavenly visitor helped you in the situation you were facing.

TOPIC

Answers From the New Testament

SYNOPSIS

Some of the most fascinating artifacts from the land of Egypt are contain-ers known as Egyptian Canopic Jars. Four of these vessels — which were purchased many years ago in the city of Aswan, Egypt — can be found on the Renner TV set. An interesting note about Aswan: it is the city where Abraham and Sarah picked up the young slave girl named Hagar.

History tells us that the Egyptians were very concerned about the after-life and how they would spend eternity. When an Egyptian died, they used canopic jars to place the organs of the deceased. There was one to hold the stomach, the lungs, the intestines, the liver, and the kidneys. The Egyptians stored the person's organs believing they would need them in the afterlife. Only the heart remained in the body; because it represented the soul of that individual, it could not be removed.

If you were to travel to Egypt today, you would not find the elaborate palaces where the Pharaohs once lived, but what you would find are highly extravagant pyramid tombs that they poured their money into building. Instead of investing the bulk of their finances in their present lives, they invested in their future ones. Although they had the right idea to invest in eternity, they didn't know how to get there, which left them eternally lost.

Thankfully, as believers, we don't need to worry about trying to preserve our earthly bodies or where we will spend eternity. When we are resur-rected to new life, we will join Jesus for eternity in Heaven and have brand new, incorruptible bodies! The question regarding our eternity has been answered!

The emphasis of this lesson:

In this lesson, Rick answers questions like: Was Joseph a carpenter? Did Jesus have brothers and sisters and grandparents? What ever happened to Pontius Pilate? What New Testament character lived in the most

expensive property in Israel? Who was the biggest philanthropist in the New Testament? And what was Paul's thorn in the flesh?

Was Joseph a Carpenter?

Matthew 13:55 says that Jesus was "the carpenter's son." The word "carpenter" used here is a very bad translation. In fact, many people have heard this and erroneously believed that carpenters were poor, but that doesn't line up with historical facts or the context of the Greek in this verse. The Greek word for "carpenter" here is *tekton*, which is from where we get the word *technology*. The word *tekton* describes *a person who is highly advanced in whatever skill he possesses* and *one who is paid a handsome salary*. It depicts *one who makes exquisite furniture, jewelry, mosaics, stone work,* or even *one who is a building supervisor*. Thus, the word "carpenter" is a very limiting, poor translation of the word *tekton*.

As a *tekton* — translated here as "carpenter" — Joseph was highly advanced in the technical skills he possessed. He was not a simple carpenter that worked with wood. Rather, he was a highly-paid professional. Although he lived in Nazareth, it is almost certain he worked as a *tekton* in the nearby city of Sepphoris, which was about three or four miles away. It was in this highly affluent town that Joseph most likely met Mary's parents and he and Mary were betrothed.

The fact that Joseph was a highly-skilled and highly-paid technician means that God entrusted Jesus to someone who had already proved himself faithful in life. When God saw Joseph, He likely said, "Now that is a man who has really managed his natural gifts well. In fact, I believe he is ready to receive a bigger assignment — the assignment to be the earthly father of My Son, Jesus."

Think about it. If God was going to give someone the greatest assignment that had ever been given in the human race — the responsibility of raising the Son of God — would He give it to someone poor and unsuccessful? Or would He entrust the task to a reliable, successful individual that had proven themselves to be trustworthy again and again? The answer is rather obvious.

Did Jesus Have Brothers and Sisters?

Many people are not aware that Jesus did have siblings and that He was not an only child. In Luke 2:7, we read that while Mary and Joseph were in Bethlehem, "...she brought forth her firstborn son, and wrapped him in swaddling clothes, and laid him in a manger; because there was no room for them in the inn." The word "firstborn" is the Greek word *prototokos*, which means *firstborn*, or *the first of other children*.

The fact that Jesus is called the "firstborn" indicates there were other children born after Him. Matthew 13:55 identifies His brothers as James, Joseph, Simon, and Jude, and verse 56 mentions He had "sisters," which means at least two sisters. When we add up all these siblings and include Jesus, it confirms that there were at least seven children in Mary and Joseph's family. Although that may come as a shock to some people, it is a biblical fact.

In this amazing family, not only do we find Jesus, the Savior of the world, but also James and Jude — two writers of books in the New Testament. So after God called Mary to be the mother of Jesus and Joseph to be His foster father, He raised up other children in that family to bring Him glory. History reveals that Joseph and Simon were also involved in ministry, and the sisters were married to people in ministry. This demonstrates how God calls entire families to His service.

Did Jesus Have Grandparents?

The fact that both Mary and Joseph had parents tells us that Jesus had grandparents, and because the Early Church writers kept such detailed history, we know quite a bit about at least two of Jesus' grandparents. For example, early records show that Mary's parents were older and had no children. They prayed for a long time for God to give them a child, and they had made a vow that if the Lord would give them a child, they would give that child to the Lord. Early Christian writers recorded that when Mary was born, her parents presented her to the Lord and dedicated her for God's service. Therefore, from the time she was an infant, the understanding of being dedicated to God was instilled into her. Moreover, her parents told her she had been born into the world to serve God. Thus, she was raised to believe that she had a *special purpose*, and she believed it.

Mary's mother — which would be Jesus' *grandmother* — was born in Jerusalem. We know this because if you go to the Pool of Bethesda, which is located on the northern side of the temple, there is a plaque on the wall that many people who visit often miss. It says, "This is where the Virgin Mary's mother was born." Furthermore, if you go down into the lowest level of that building, you will find the First-Century house where Mary's mother was born. Thus, Jesus' grandparents lived in Jerusalem.

Now, we know from historical records that Mary's parents — who would have been Jesus' grandparents — later moved to the city of Sepphoris where there was a large synagogue. Mary's father became a *scroll scholar* there, which means he served in full-time ministry and his life was built around a commitment to the Scriptures. As the overseer of the sacred scrolls, he served in the local "church." At some point in Mary's young life, her father and her family relocated to Nazareth, but her father continued to serve as the keeper of the sacred scrolls in the city of Sepphoris.

Sepphoris was a city of great magnificence and beauty and a major center of religious learning. In fact, it was so important that when Jerusalem fell to the Romans in 70 AD, all religious education moved from Jerusalem to the city of Sepphoris. Jesus' life and ministry were strongly influenced by this city. He had spent ample time there visiting with His grandparents, and He likely worked side-by-side with His father, Joseph, when He was older. His exposure to the enormous wealth of the city, as well as the banking industry and the theater, gave Him many analogies and ideas about money and life that He would never have seen in Nazareth. This explains why Jesus was able to speak with such knowledge and authority on a wide range of subjects that He would have never been privy to in Nazareth.

All these intricate details about Jesus' grandparents and the influence of the town where they lived tell us why God chose Mary. His ways are not strange and mysterious like some people say. In many ways, He is very logical and even predictable in how He works. Nothing He does is accidental or by random chance. Mary was raised in a home where the Word of God was honored. She had heard the prophecies of the coming Messiah from the time she was a little girl and was trained to hear God's voice. Accordingly, when He revealed His will to her through Gabriel — that she had been chosen to be the mother of the Messiah — she accepted it without deep struggle. She had been intentionally prepared by her parents and taught to serve God faithfully — explicitly obeying whatever God asked her to do. This shows the importance of dedicating your children — and grandchildren — to the Lord. It is never too late to commit your family to the Lord's care and service.

What Ever Happened to Pontius Pilate?

For the entire span of Jesus' three-year ministry, Pilate was governor of Judea. He was the supreme authority in all legal matters throughout the entire territory. The region of Judea made up a large portion of the land of Israel, and it was ruled by a Roman-appointed procurator or governor. It was an extremely unstable environment. Because of the constant revolts in Jerusalem and Judea, most governors only lasted for one to three years and were then replaced. This was not the case for Pontius Pilate. He ruled Judea with an iron fist for 10 years. This fact shows just how cruel and ruthless he was and is confirmed by noted historian Flavius Josephus.

There was a document produced in the 19th Century called the *Archko Volume* (or the *Archko Library*), which included alleged reports that Pilate had converted to Christianity before his death. Although this writing was widely popular for a number of years, it is a total fraudulent piece of so-called ancient literature. If you've ever read it, don't believe a word of it.

Ultimately, there were so many complaints against Pilate that reached the ears of Caesar that Pilate fell out of favor with Rome. The emperor eventually released him from his duties and exiled him to Gaul, which is modern-day France. Historians say that in the end, Pilate committed suicide. This brutal man who lived a tragic life played a very pivotal role in the life of Jesus and the role of history.

What New Testament Character Lived in the Most Expensive Property in Israel?

Early Church writings tell us that Joseph of Arimathea was the brother of Mary's father, which would make him Mary's uncle and Jesus' great uncle. Of all the inhabitants of the land of Israel, Joseph of Arimathea was the wealthiest man, and he lived on the most expensive piece of property. He was not a government official or a member of royalty. He was simply a relative of Mary, and he became the guardian of Jesus and His family after Joseph died.

Scholars believe that he likely managed the abundant resources given to Jesus by the Magi after Joseph's passing. This may explain why during Jesus' ministry there is no record that He ever took an offering. He always had all the money He needed to do ministry — He even had a full time treasurer. This also explains why the Bible says that Jesus was buried in a rich man's tomb. It was the freshly-hewn sepulcher of Joseph of Arimathea, His great uncle.

Who Was the Biggest Philanthropist in the New Testament?

While Joseph of Arimathea was the wealthiest man in Israel, Jesus holds the record of being the biggest philanthropist in the New Testament. Acts 10:38 says, "…God anointed Jesus of Nazareth with the Holy Ghost and with power: who went about doing good, and healing all that were oppressed of the devil; for God was with him."

There is a very interesting phrase in this verse that most people misunderstand. The words "who went about doing good" is not just a description of the healing and deliverance Jesus brought to people. It is actually a translation of a Greek word that was exclusively used to describe *a person who did philanthropic work*. This included feeding the poor, clothing the needy, and treating the sick. This means that in addition to Jesus providing spiritual restoration, He also met people's physical needs.

As we noted, Jesus had a tremendous supply of resources available to Him, and He used His finances to feed the hungry and clothe the naked — both naturally and spiritually. This tells us that in addition to providing spiritual nourishment and healing, we need to provide physical nourishment and care as well. What Jesus did is what we are to do.

Why Did Jesus Give the Apostles Power To Tread Upon Serpents and Scorpions?

In Luke 10:19, Jesus said, "Behold, I give unto you power to tread on serpents and scorpions, and over all the power of the enemy: and nothing shall by any means hurt you." When Jesus sent out His disciples to preach the Gospel, there were many primitive roads in those days that were very difficult to travel. Deep ruts, dangerous rocks, and perilous holes were a constant hazard, not to mention the places where there were no roads, and the disciples had to blaze their own trail through dense brush.

Equally important is the fact that this region of the Middle East was filled with dangerous snakes and scorpions that were a serious threat to travelers. When Jesus spoke the promise of Luke 10:19, He was guaranteeing divine protection for all who go out and preach and teach the Gospel. There was no need to worry or be anxious or fearful about snakes or scorpions or any other hazard they would encounter.

Also notice the word "over" in this verse. It is the Greek word *epi*, and it carries the idea of *superiority*. By using this word, Jesus declared to His disciples — both then and now — that it doesn't matter what the devil tries to do to us, because we have been given a position of superiority over everything he throws our way. This divine ability to crush every pestilence under our feet is just as active today as it was when Jesus spoke it two thousand years ago!

What Was Paul's Thorn in the Flesh?

In Second Corinthians 12:7, the apostle Paul said, "And lest I should be exalted above measure through the abundance of the revelations, there was given to me a thorn in the flesh, the messenger of Satan to buffet me, lest I should be exalted above measure." The question of what Paul's "thorn in the flesh" was has been a topic of great debate for many years. There are some who claim his thorn was an eye disease. Others have said it was that Paul had clubbed feet. But neither of these is supported by Scripture or the writings of the Early Church.

Then there are others who say Paul had an issue of pride because of the many revelations God had given him. But that isn't necessarily true. When you really have a revelation from God, it is a very humbling experience. The Bible says the wisdom that comes from heaven is pure, peaceable, and gentle (*see* James 3:17). True revelations from God tend to instill the fear of the Lord in us, not pride.

If we remain true to the context of Scripture, we'll see the answer to what Paul's thorn in the flesh was is rather obvious. Paul said, "And lest I should be exalted above measure through the abundance of the revelations, there was given to me a thorn in the flesh, the messenger of Satan to buffet me..." (2 Corinthians 12:7).

Basically, Paul said, "You know, I could really make headway and affect many new regions because of all the amazing revelations God has given me. But because they are so impactful and transforming, there was given to me a thorn in the flesh." When most people read, "There was given me," they think the thorn in the flesh came from God, but the verse doesn't say that. In fact, Paul tells us where the "thorn" came from — it is "the messenger of Satan." The on-going struggle Paul was experiencing came from the devil, and the words "there was given me" would better be translated *"there was assigned to me."*

Paul was dealing with some kind of a demonic force that had been assigned to "buffet" him. This word "buffet" means *to beat, to hinder, to hamper, or to distract.* Why did Paul have a demonic assignment against him? He said, "Lest I should be exalted above measure." In other words, "For fear that I should break into new realms and affect more people with the Gospel, a messenger from Satan was sent to hamper me."

What was Paul's thorn in the flesh? It was *a messenger of Satan.* To be specific, it was *people* —Judaizers, legalizers, and false brethren that attacked him everywhere he went. They "buffeted" him, hassled him, and were a distraction to him. If he hadn't had to deal with harassing people, just think of how much more progress he might have made. But he had to deal with them all the time.

In response to these ongoing attacks, Paul said, "For this thing I besought the Lord thrice, that it might depart from me. And he said unto me, My grace is sufficient for thee: for my strength is made perfect in weakness..." (2 Corinthians 12:8,9).

Paul's prayer to remove the messenger of Satan was a prayer God could not answer. Think about it: Paul was saying, "God, would You please remove all these problematic people from my life." The fact is, if God removed one person, the devil would just send another one. The same is true for you. If you pray and God removes the aggravating person you're struggling with, the devil will just send another one — and another one and another one. God can't remove all the problematic people in your life, but He will give you the power to deal with them and overcome. That is why God told Paul, "My grace will show up in you, right in the middle of your struggle."

So Paul's thorn in the flesh was not an eye disease, clubbed feet, or pride. It was people. If you find yourself struggling with people, always remember that someone once struggled with you. We're all imperfect. Rather than pray, "God, remove all these problematic people from my life," just say, "Lord, give me the grace (power) to forgive these people, deal with

these people, and overcome the ungodly spirits working through them."
And He will give you the grace you need — just like he did for Paul.

STUDY QUESTIONS

**Study to shew thyself approved unto God, a workman that needeth
not to be ashamed, rightly dividing the word of truth.
— 2 Timothy 2:15**

1. What is the greatest eye-opening fact that you learned about Jesus
   and his parents, grandparents, and siblings? How do the details in this
   lesson about Jesus' family expand your understanding of His home life
   and His ability to identify with and relate to the dynamics of being
   human?

2. Isn't it interesting that there is no record in Scripture that Jesus ever
   collected an offering? He always had the money and resources He
   needed to minister and carry out the assignment the Father had given
   Him. What does this say to you about fulfilling God's call on *your*
   life? (As you answer, consider Second Corinthians 9:8-11; Philippians
   4:19; Psalm 84:11.)

3. As the New Testament's biggest philanthropist, Jesus not only met
   people's spiritual needs, He also met their physical needs. Take a few
   moments to look up First John 3:16-18 in a few different versions of
   the Bible. What is the Holy Spirit speaking to you through this passage? Write out the version of verse 18 that is most impactful to you.

PRACTICAL APPLICATION

**But be ye doers of the word, and not hearers only,
deceiving your own selves.
— James 1:22**

1. Mary had been intentionally prepared by her parents and taught
   to serve God faithfully from the earliest age. What are you doing
   specifically to hide the Word of God in the hearts of your children (or
   grandchildren) and prepare them to serve God? What kind of results
   is it producing? Is there anything different you sense the Holy Spirit
   is prompting you to do with them? If so, what is it?

2. History reveals that God called every member of Jesus' family into ministry. In what ways are you and your family serving God at church, in the community, at work, and elsewhere?

3. Paul's "thorn in the flesh" was a messenger of Satan. Specifically, it was problematic people sent to hinder, harass, and distract Paul from his calling. Are you dealing with problematic people? Instead of praying for God to remove them from your life, pray, "Lord, give me the grace (power) to forgive these people, deal with these people, and overcome the ungodly spirits working through them. In Jesus' name. Amen."

Notes